THIS LITTLE LIGHT

LISA SUNSHINE

ABOUT LISA

Lisa is funny, down to earth and a ray of sunshine. She is a FB blogger, radio personality, certified life coach, and most importantly, a HOPE DEALER. She has overcome years of childhood trauma, poverty, domestic violence, homelessness and just recently,
the loss of their 17 year old son, Kalen.

Her purpose in life is to inspire every person she meets to rise above their plight and ignite a fire in every person to dream again and "DESIGN YOUR LIFE". Her mission is to encourage each person to pray, write down their vision and execute the plan with wisdom and a blessed assurance that what each of us has to offer is
LIFE BREATHING for someone else.

Lisa is a bold visionary who surrounds herself with great life influencers who believe and KNOW first hand, with God all things are possible. Her goal is to hear from, speak to and empower women and the people who love them.

DEDICATION

A heartfelt amount of love and gratitude to my husband, Dwayne Johnson (The REAL Tony Kirk, Sr), our children, Lexy, Tony, Sierra, Emeri, Langston, Kalen and Kennedy.

Your pain has been my pain, your rewards have been my joys. Each of you have taught me so much. I am wealthy because of you. Mom, our recovery process continues. I am blessed every day as we get better at loving each other.

To my siblings, Althea, Vickie, and Contessa, I have a great appreciation for sisterhood. It's all because of you three. Dana, words can't convey how much your little sister adores you.

To my god children, Lexi II, London and Ray Jr, your lives in mine is a blessing from God. To the Inner Circle, you are priceless. To my editor and amazing friend, Nada, you rock, woman!

To each of you, thank you for letting your light bless my light. May we all make the world a better place to live out our purpose. May our legacy be rich in joy, peace and charity. - Lisa D.

INTRODUCTION

Lisa Kirk's journey is filled with *my* story, the good, the bad as well as the life lessons that make me who I am today. You will find quotes, jokes, scriptures, letters to myself and poetic pieces within these pages. This book is the first in a series of five. You will find assignments for you to complete as you read each chapter. The assignments will help IF you do the work. Many of you are like me. We believe time is precious, and there is no time for waiting any longer to overturn the pain so that it can work for your good! Are you wondering about your purpose? Are you trying to find purpose in your pain? Questions like, "Why was I born if abuse is all I endure?" Or, "What is wrong with me that my own parents don't love and take care of me?" Are you seeking affirmation in all the wrong places? Do you need to make peace with your past? Are you still heavy laden with unforgiveness? My prayer is to encourage you through reading about the hell I endured and overcame. I pray you will find your BEAUTIFUL place as you journey through my memoir. Please, take your time with this work. Your healing is no longer a mystery, but an attainable ray of light waiting to be visualized and experienced. This new place is a place that is peaceful, kind, forgiving and full of purpose. Your spectacular, intricately woven purpose has YOU written all over it! You have made it this far because you were created in purpose. Every time you got back up after a bad experience or debilitating attack, that was your little light pulling and tugging on you to GET BACK UP again. The world can be so dark and lonely. Working through heartbreak and despair can be scary. Being stuck in despair and unforgiveness is even scarier. This book is about moving from darkness to light. It is a snapshot of how, when the work of recovery is complete, your freedom shows up. Once you recover and SHINE, the darkness that had you bound is diminished. And that is the ultimate goal - much more light, less and less darkness. *This Little Light* is encouragement for the individual who cannot seem to understand that what they already own is ENOUGH. This memoir is a WAKE-UP call to anyone who needs to know that you can go through the darkness of pain and suffering yet have a gem of sunshine within you to recover and conquer your past. The weight of glory within you is enough. The Light of Christ is greater than anything the world can ever thrust upon you. If you do the work of recovery, your own little light will be the spark to create the life you've always wanted but couldn't seem to get a handle on. If, like me, you could never answer the door when death called for you, that is because the attacks always bowed down to the power of God within you. This mantle of helping others heal has been within me for decades, but first, my personal healing had to manifest. My assignment to inspire people to heal and share with those who are ready to launch from a place of brokenness, came with PAIN first. Birth brought my purpose, then came the life of pain. Years later, my wholeness and liberation are here, and my life's work is in full bloom. Now, the time has come for your healing. It is absolutely OKAY to be in pain right now. The question is, are you ready to begin your healing journey? The reality of your future is beautiful if you are willing to work for it. This memoir is to help you realize your recovery.

You are WELL ABLE TO SLAY THIS GIANT. It is your turn to INSPIRE and REACH others to share with those you were destined to IGNITE. But first, recognize your own little light and how significant it is. Don't discount it. Your light is enough. Your time has finally come to live beautifully, authentically, and filled with a "CAN DO IT" mindset. Own that mindset and let it bless your life, not once, but for all.

PREFACE

To the one who was left to carry the weight of being an adult when you were just a child, I see you. I want to acknowledge the presence of you who was abused and left vulnerable by those who were supposed to protect you. I see you too! And to those who were neglected and criticized, mocked and bullied, ostracized and never fit in, I acknowledge you as well. The once bruised and broken one, the one with scars that remain, that are now emotional and deep, but were once seeable, I recognize you too. To the adopted one, never knowing your origin, but accepting the void and living like it didn't matter, when it does even more today, I acknowledge your presence here. I pray while you are reading this book that you will experience a peace and joy YOU HAVE NEVER KNOWN. I pray that hope rises within you so that you can begin to see clearly as the pain goes away. Let the refreshing grace of God flow through every painful place and bring you out of agony - prepared to go beyond what you have endured, into purpose with clarity. Allow all I have been through and overcome to be the blessing you have prayed for: HOPE and INSPIRATION. May you see yourself in the future, looking better than you do right now.

To you all, I say this - YOU ARE NOW IN CHARGE. Gone are the days of abuse and rejection. That pain was then - TODAY'S A NEW DAY, and I am your RAY OF SUNSHINE showing up because Jesus is the light that shineth in me! What I know today I surely could have used long ago through the years. Now that I do know a few things, I will use them until I can't use them any longer. What I know I will share, and what I share will be for the rebuilding of you, the beautiful ones, who once were me, surely! I survived, I overcame, I forgave, I prayed - I FOUND ME so that I could help you find you. I forgave the pain so that I could finally live free to be ALL OF ME, not a shadow of myself, but every bit of the sunshine on a cloudy day, when it's cold outside even IF it ain't the month of May, I shine. And when I shine, truth is, you shine. When we shine, we GLOW to reflect a better way, a sweeter, much kinder way to live and be. Free! You are free to change what has not worked. Free to rid your psyche of each and EVERY belittling word, every jab to your flesh, and every word left unspoken. You are free to HEAL. The hope of glory is available to you. Let that hope have its way completely.

Go ahead, think about it. Think back on your life for a little while. Write down a list of every weight that has left you limping or even stuck and crippled, like that dude at the pool who was there for 38 years (John 5:1-18). How long has it been? How long have you wanted so desperately to be free from it all? How long have you waited for another person to HELP YOU into the pool to receive your healing? My question for you today is, "Do you REALLY want to be well, or has limping become your comfort zone?"

How each of us came through our hard place may be different, but I am willing to bet your right arm, our healing journey will look quite similar. Most of us want the same things: Things like wealth, a beautiful home, a loving family, a great career. Most of us truly long for all of the above. We want love, peace, joy, purpose and CLARITY. We want togetherness in our families, a unified family that loves, forgives and supports one another. We pray for a healthy life: Spirit, soul and body. It is when we get down to attaining all these things that life happens. Choices, decisions (others and ours), both good and bad, begin to shape us long before we even have a choice to choose how we will live and love. For many of us, life chose our path and we went along for the ride and stayed seated as a passenger way beyond the pain of realizing just how jacked up we had become. Many of you remain there. Waiting - at the pool.

BLENDED AND BROKEN

⁂

I can remember feeling so empty. I had a sixth sense before I knew what intuition or discernment meant. I was five years old and my mom wasn't there. She left us with our grandmother and a family friend in Montgomery, Alabama. Mom and soon-to-be bonus dad, went to scout things out in Florida because it would eventually become our new home. I was sick to my stomach because I didn't know where I belonged. I felt afraid and unsafe. Our grandmother lived three homes from us, so the four of us kids went between grandma's house and ours. Mom left us with a family friend who turned out not to be so friendly. This friend was irresponsible and unsafe. She should have never been given permission to watch us for the week or, so my mom was away. Our bonus dad was a single father of three teenage boys. Boys who were much older than all of us, especially me, the baby of the family. With no one to look out for us at our home, and grandmother quite comfortable in her home, things happened at our house that created the makings of a perfect storm.

We moved to Clearwater and things were confusing. There were A LOT of new people who became our family. They were funny, strange, very loud and loved to drink and do drugs. I didn't learn until much later in life that our family was extremely dysfunctional and TOXIC in so many ways. Poverty, ignorance, alcohol and drug abuse, and very few, if any safeguards for the children was the lifestyle. There was nothing normal about how we lived. We didn't have our own home or private space for quite some time. Strange things happen to children when adults are busy being irresponsible adults. Lurkers are on the prowl for their victims. Horrible, physically painful and extremely shameful things happened. A lifetime of scars was created during those years. Scars that can't be seen today, but the residue is ever present. Due to my dad being so "protective" of his girls, I knew he would kill the person who did such atrocious things. Because things were already bad enough, I felt horrible at the thought of me making our lives worse by telling on the demon who was hurting me. I didn't want my mom to be even more stressed than she already was. Unfortunately, pedophiles "groom" the innocence from children. They say things to bring them into their demonic world and then take their innocence without guilt or conscience. That very thing happened in our home time and time again.

∿

MY BONUS DAD WAS THE OLDEST OF HIS SIBLINGS AND THEY RELIED on him heavily for all sorts of things. Things like money, handy man stuff (he was a licensed electrician) and dealing with relatives who were out of control. One thing was certain, our bonus dad loved us. He showed us how to cook really outlandish German dishes and simple, but delicious American food as well. He learned how to cook these meals as a soldier in the United States Army. He was an all-around likable guy who cursed a lot and worked a lot! What was really crazy is that he was a hair dresser too and was very good at it. He did our "jerry curls", trims and such like a pro! He loved his family and loved to joke around in a nice way, most of the time. He also LOVED playing chess and watching Star Trek. My daily job was to help him take off his work boots and get him a Schlitz Malt Liquor Bull beer as soon as he got in the door from work. I played with his lighter, a lot, and it burned my fingers. His favorite cigarettes were Carlton Menthol 100's. Back then he had to write a note for me to buy his cigarettes. In those days you could tell an adult's hand writing from a child's. Mom came home angry most days, exhausted, at best. She didn't like her job at the cigar factory in downtown Clearwater. She liked her co-workers, but the job was stressful. She and all the others on the "floor" of the factory got paid by the number of cigars they rolled each day. She hated when the foreman would purposely slow down the machines. Mom graduated with her GED because she had my sister at 16 years old. At some point, my mother and grandmother were pregnant at the same time. My grandmother beat my mom so badly, the scar is still there. She was so angry at my mom for getting pregnant at 15 years old. Years later, that same anger would find its way to our home. My mom was handed a curse that she wasn't even aware of and one that she didn't know how to eradicate. Our way of life was "the way things were done back then is good enough for now." In the old days, children were "seen and not heard", told what to do, as "the help." Children, for the most part, weren't honored and respected or seen as a blessing, but made to feel like a burden. And as soon as you could help out financially, your money was TAKEN from you before you could count it. At least in our house that's how things happened. We were told where to get on and off, when to come in and out, how to cook, what to eat and how to clean and smell good. The elders of my family always looked very nice. That's when southern belles were nicely dressed and prissy. When gentlemen wore suits and ties and fedoras. To this day, I give honor to my mom, grandmother, great aunts and older cousins for teaching me how a lady should dress.

Mom could sing really, really, well. She made the people at church shout every time she was on the microphone. I never lived with my biological dad but was told that he was an incredible dancer and a drum major at Sidney Lanier in Montgomery. My creative gifts, even interior design, is a family thing. My grandmother was an upholsterer and a ceramics maker. My two sisters and I would spend the summers with my grandmother. My brother stayed at home to help our dad with odd jobs, plus, he was a football player. Conditioning in the gym took place every summer so he couldn't get away like us girls. EVERY hot summer in Montgomery was an adventure, although we felt like our skin would sweat off our bodies because it was so hot. There were only two air conditioners in grandma's house. One in the living room for company and one in the back den for us when we watched, like clockwork, The Price Is Right, Ryan's Hope, All My Children, Young & The Restless, As the World Turns and Guiding Light. Between Ericka Kane, Victor Newman, Josh and Reva, along with the philanthropic and never dying Spauldings, our summers were BUSY tuned into daytime soap operas. I could write an entire chapter on soap operas in the 80s. We had a ball laughing and crying every single week day, hanging onto every word that preceded out of the mouths of our favorite daytime stars. The "soaps" struggle was real! My grandmother scheduled our lives around the daily television line up. We had to go to the laundry mat, pay bills downtown or go grocery shopping on the base, all based on being back home by the time Bob Barker was yelling, "... and you're the next contestant onnnnnnnnnn, the Price Is Right!!!!!!" Grandma was a military widow and she made her fixed income work. She made sure we knew who Rosa Parks was, and why it was important to ride the bus and sit in the front of the bus. She had a perfectly good working car, but we rode that city bus nearly everywhere but church and doctor's appointments, and appointments weren't all off the hook. If her appointments on the air force base were early enough in the morning or late enough in the afternoon, her car would sit right there, and we would hop on that bus like it was Uber. Grandma would put on her Estee Lauder body powder, lotion her hands with Avon branded lotion and grease her scalp with blue Royal Crown and strut her stuff like she was royalty. She would take us to the hair school for a trim and pressing at least once per summer. She knew we were struggling in Florida, so she did what she could to help prepare us for the upcoming school year. She and a very dear cousin went in together to buy our school clothes. She also bought us really pretty outfits for the 4th of July, when all our relatives would come from all over to barbeque and sit around and talk about old times. My great uncles could sing and cook. And my goodness, how they could barbeque ANYTHING. My Uncle Mutt taught me how to cut up a chicken even though my hands were small. I felt like a gourmet chef after that lesson. We may have moved away while I was young, but Montgomery is home for us. We visit often and take pride in all the invaluable history that took place there. During my formative years, Montgomery was my safe haven.

NO ONE TO TRUST

T he enemy of our souls has no care or concern for age or innocence. Due to my mom's upbringing and her lack of knowing any better, she beat us just like her mom beat her. There was no safe place for me. I didn't think I could tell my mom because when she was upset, she would call us bad names and tell me I better not be "acting fast!" Between her rage and my innocence being taken by a very unsuspecting family member, I had no one to turn to for help. My attacker knew how enraged my dad would be if he found out. The more my mom would beat me, the more my childhood innocence was taken. Even as a young person, I knew I was BRILLIANT. Unfortunately, I died to my brokenness EVERY DAY. There was never a day I didn't wish I were dead. Remember the perfect storm I spoke of earlier? This was it. My grandmother already hated our dad with a passion. She knew he did drugs and she hated him for taking us away from her, so telling my grandma was totally out of the realm of possibilities. Mom says moving to Florida was the best thing for us at that time. Montgomery was really stuck in segregation and it showed. Clearwater was very different, very tropical, very bright, and we were outdoors a lot. I HATED being in the house. It was very, very rare that our home was a safe place. I stayed away as much as possible, and I stayed at church as much as I could. I was involved in every activity I could participate in. I was in the youth choir, served as an usher, and attended Sunday School faithfully. That was until I met the love of my life, or so I dreamed. He was a toxic teenaged guy, and I was a toxic teenaged girl. You know the rest. We experienced what every relationship experiences when two really immature and broken people are together. We experienced pain at its very core. We created a crazy, mixed up life together - then we got married. I will spare you the gory details of that union for my next book. Just know that manipulation, pride, coping mechanisms, the pain of generational curses, abortion, lies, infidelity, domestic violence, and betrayal were every bit a part of our pre-marital and married life. The truth is, we tainted everything we touched, and it remained that way until I began my healing journey. I was a victim of domestic violence only once. From there, I was no longer a victim because I CHOSE TO REMAIN. I wasn't placed in physical chains, nor was I threatened with a deadly weapon. My spirit, soul and body were my personal weapons of mass destruction. Destruction happened consistently until the day I changed my mind. I got SICK and TIRED of placing my life and future in the hands of people who were just as broken as I was, if not worse. The day came when I turned my spirit, soul and body into weapons of BLESSED CONSTRUCTION.

～

THIS IS THE TRUTH:

Children are innocent and should never be made to feel unprotected by their parents or guardians. Children weren't asked to be born. They aren't little adults who have a background or amount of experience that will prevent them from doing what children do. Children need healthy parents. Yes, mom and dad are needed to fulfill the purpose and plan for parenting. Unhealthy parents train, by their lifestyles, unhealthy children who then turn into unhealthy young adults. If changes don't happen, the curse remains all the way into adulthood. The way in which an individual's one unhealthy person can contaminate from youth to adulthood is absolutely astonishing. If you are in the habit of saying demeaning things to your child(ren) please, please stop that behavior immediately. Parents, you are setting your child up for the same type of life that you have displayed. If you are abusing (not spanking), STOP that behavior and do like I did, seek clinical counseling. I felt I was on a different path because I didn't abuse my children, physically; but emotionally, I traumatized my two oldest daughters because I mimicked what happened at home during my childhood. The truth is, children mimic consistency/habits, as well as speech. Please remember there are two aspects of healing, one is clinical, and one is spiritual. DO BOTH to heal well and remain well. Whatever you do, do not stop until you UNLEARN what does not work and LEARN what is beneficial to everyone in your household. Take a parenting class. Seek out and KEEP a mentor to help you become a parent who SHOWS LOVE and provides LOGIC. Once you get the help you need, make sure to get support for your child(ren). It will not sit well to hear your child say things about you, but if those things are true, be real about it and apologize. If you are embarrassed by what you did, say it, "I am so embarrassed that I did that." Be transparent enough to show that you are sorry and willing to learn to do better as a parent. Then, FORGIVE YOURSELF. Move forward with a changed mind and heart. Do not say, "Well, it happened to me too" and do not make excuses. Let them know that no matter what they were told, whatever happened to them as a child, was NOT their fault. Let your child know that you wish things were different and you would have done a better job at protecting them. If you have young children at home, be careful who you allow around them. Family members are the closest to your children. PLEASE KNOW: KEEP YOUR EYES ON YOUR CHILDREN, especially when around family. Children are harmed by relatives 80% more than by a stranger. It makes sense, they have proximity to our children because families gather together. If you have failed in this area, show your remorse and ask your child for forgiveness. Lastly, what healthy boundaries need to be created to have a healthy relationship with your child, even if they are an adult? This vital life skill is a LEARNED habit. Research the book, *Boundaries*, by Henry Cloud and John Townsend. The book will BLESS YOUR LIFE once you read it. Make sure you use it and it will provide much needed answers and HELP for you as well as those around you.

ASK: WHAT WORK DO I NEED TO DO?

A.

B.

C.

D.

WHAT AREA(S) DO I NEED TO IMPROVE ON AS IT RELATES TO apologizing and forgiveness?

A.

B.

C.

D.

WHAT ARE MY TAKEAWAYS FROM THIS CHAPTER?

A.

B.

C.

D.

CHOOSE THE BLESSING

Y ou have the choice to NEVER BE BOUND AGAIN. Free yourself by releasing the pain and agony of BLAMING. Release the mindset of being a victim. It serves no useful purpose and has debilitated millions of people for far too long. Yes, you were hurt. YES, it was horrible and so painful. NO ONE should ever make light of a child being sexually abused, physically traumatized or verbally attacked, especially if those things happened at the hands of a parent or someone else who should have covered and protected the child. Today, if never before, you are VALIDATED. Your validation was sealed the moment God allowed your heart to start beating. He formed you for THIS MOMENT. I know, isn't that amazing? You fought the good fight all these years to get to this place. The air is clearer now that shame cannot remain. Know that you can write your letter and SPEAK YOUR TRUTH. Mail it to the person who hurt you or burn it as a sign that what was done to you is OVER, and the life you create now in this new season will be THE BEST LIFE YOU HAVE EVER LIVED. The truth of what happened should not define you. Your pain journey can cease TODAY, regardless of what happened to you. You now have the keys to close every hurtful door and open every blessed window. Accept that you have work to do to get the results you desire. Next, bless your life by FULLY understanding that your life will be better once YOU DO THE WORK of healing COMPLETELY. Can you imagine the number of people who would have remained broken and bitter had Oprah never shared her story? Think about the number of people she has employed throughout her career. Remember, Oprah was raped at nine years old and gave birth at 14 years old. Her baby died weeks later. She shared her story AFTER she did the work of healing and forgiving. Today, Oprah is one of the top grossing female billionaires on the planet. Will your story help millions like Oprah's? Probably not. But if one person's life is made better because of you, let that possibility be one of your inspirations. May the most important inspiration be the simple fact that you are sick and tired of living beneath your God- given privilege.

THE HEALING POWER OF WORDS

W hile it seems like words jump off the pages of books and magazines we read, it is hearts that are CHANGED when we receive those words of affirmation and hope. It almost feels like we have permission to heal. That permission seems so unattainable when freedom happens in our minds, but actually, it is the truth that sets us free, so we can finally change our minds and DO SOMETHING ABOUT what happened to and IN us. I have always had a way with words, so in 2013, I began a journal/blog. Today, you get to read those words that poured from my soul. I pray you allow them to permeate your thoughts and inspire you to have a made-up mind to BE FREE from your past. I pray you are moved in such a way that you GET UP and LIVE A BLESSED and PEACE-FILLED life. A life that is full and rich, a life poured out because now, for the first time, you are filled to overflow. Filled up with goodness, kindness, grace and mercy and a MADE-UP MIND to go on with God as your help and a new pep in your step. You can move ahead knowing YOUR SUNSHINE IS ENOUGH and the GIFTS GO WHERE YOU GO. You no longer need to be fixed or approved because you know WHO created you and WHY.

REMEMBER, WHILE YOU'RE LOOKING FOR THE BEST THERE IS, START with you. Because you, *you* are the answer to someone's prayer. Long gone are the days when you need to be validated. Say so long to the days of yearning for attention from people who need the same thing you yearned for. Understand that you are the reason why someone won't fail. Today, finally understand and accept that God created you for such a time as this to GO FORTH and BE GREAT. Lastly, always know this: You and God are a majority. Everything else pales in comparison.

-LISA SUNSHINE

BLOG, SHARE AND HEAL

⤫

M y process of healing started on:

MAY 9, 2013

Life has a way of blowing us away - sometimes for the good! Today, in honor of my BIGGEST motivator and "live your dreams" champion, I will honor my baby girl, Kennedy, by starting my new journal/blog! I didn't really plan it this way, but when I got up this morning I prayed that I would live my BEST LIFE and that I would not miss ANY divine appointments! Today, Kennedy's 11th birthday, will go down in the history books!

You see, Kennedy tells me almost EVERY DAY that I should be on this TV show or in this magazine, or I could write a book and it would be on the best-seller's book stand...and she believes I CAN! That's what I love about her, she sincerely BELIEVES in her Mommy :-) Don't get me wrong, this little lady is brutally honest. This lil girl doesn't believe I can keep my closet clean for two weeks straight, or that I could have only two browsers on my laptop at one time (I normally have about 12...lol. And the one I really love...Kennedy doesn't believe I can keep a straight FACE when I'm irritated! I'll post faces another day, so you know what the deal is!

Please pray with me as I blog to inspire YOU TO LIVE - not just exist like a rubber tree plant, but be ALIVE, be PRESENT, be INTENTIONAL, be ACTIVE, be LOYAL and be BEAUTIFUL! TODAY.

~

May 9, 2013

I had very, very, very humble beginnings - think PLASTIC spoon NOT PLATINUM. At some point years ago, I decided I had had enough of mediocre living. Mediocrity is pitiful, really. What's worse is knowing you were created to BE MORE, yet you allow the harsh realities of life to SMOTHER your dreams and great mind. I began this ugly and backward metamorphosis - I was living up to the expectations of others - of people who didn't even like me (surely, you've never done that).

But then, there's the INCREDIBLE power of PRAYER and knowing what God says about you! Can I get a "whoop there it is"? That single moment led to more minutes, then hours that led into days of "speaking life" to myself! I became my own encourager and motivator! By myself. Alone. Individual. Just Me. Not a group of people going with me, or even two or three encouragers - just Lisa.

Check this out: You will be the only person doing that ONE particular thing because you were created to do it. Relish the truth about yourself: ONLY YOU CAN DO IT! It was mind blowing that God would think so highly of ME - this lil girl born in Tuskegee, Alabama, who's never had a 5- minute conversation with her own father. The one who had a baby her senior year in high school, survived domestic violence, and married three times. The one who made horrible choices time after time after time...BUT, He did. He chose me to do GREAT THINGS in this life that I was blessed with! ...and I WILL.

~

MAY 9, 2013

My spirit, soul and body were created to endure and overcome! Trying to be someone else or looking like someone else is such a great waste of time! I am fearfully and wonderfully made...all of me! Yep, even the parts that look like I eat more ribs and cheesecake than pink grapefruit and celery sticks! Ha! I know my worth. I know my destiny is SURE, and no matter what crazy thoughts try to invade my mind or tell me I am not good enough, those thoughts cannot take root. I WILL LIVE MY LIFE to the fullest!!!!

My thoughts are creative, life-changing and helpful. I have the power to create wealth and destroy DEBT - not just for me, but for others as well!

Even today, I am about to go out and make somebody's day! Imagine what life would be like if we didn't know how to SPEAK LIFE to ourselves???? Imagine the millions who DON'T.

"I tried being normal. It was the worst five minutes of my life!"

~

MAY 13, 2013

My Monday Morning Truth:

Times of refreshing come when you take time out to be refreshed! You can only truly give from your OVERFLOW. How can you live your BEST life if you won't take the much-needed time to pray, write down your goals, and create a plan of action that includes a measure of phenomenal results? Time and chance happen to each one of us every day. CRAP HAPPENS too. No one gets to be the exception to THAT rule. Things happen beyond our control.

Kids get sick, the washer/dryer stop working, you may get *a phone call with bad news*...BUT, trouble don't last always. When you bounce back, what do you return to? Same old thing, just a different day? I don't think so. Life is crazy UNLESS YOU make it beautiful!

If you won't PLAN YOUR BLESSED FUTURE, it won't happen. Just think about your life over the past month. Have you gone to work without a list of things to be accomplished? Have you gone to school without a lesson plan or list of course work that needed to be completed? If you have, please, by all means, HIT THE RE-SET BUTTON because you are in the wrong lane! Wishing on a star is NOT how it's done ladies and gentlemen! If you don't have a well-thought-out plan to refer back to when life knocks you down, how do you recover? Creating resources once life hits IS NOT the time. We all must be WELL-equipped with the right tools when life happens. Life is much too precious to leave to chance. Make plans today - and make sure they are HUGE! IT IS YOUR LIFE WE'RE TALKING ABOUT HERE!!!! You are handiwork created by the greatest HANDY MAN EVER! ACT LIKE YOU KNOW!

Make sure your plans are so huge that you cannot do it by yourself. Take the Lord and a few cool folks with you, and you are sure to SEE your plans come to fruition.

～

MAY 13, 2013

Odd Ball In: Part 1

Have you ever put on an outfit or a pair of shoes and just didn't feel comfortable? Or maybe been at work or among a group of people and felt like the TOTAL ODD BALL? For years I absolutely hated my life!

I was too white to be black, as some would say, and too black to be white - I didn't fit in anywhere! I would be talked about by so- called friends and totally shunned by others. Even now, people will say, "What ARE you?" And for the life of me, I HAVE TO HAVE FUN WITH THEIR QUESTION! My responses sometimes have me laughing for days. You see, I was living with the void of not having a relationship with my father, seeing my mother go through struggle after struggle, PLUS I'm the baby of my mom's four children - we're at minimum, three years apart and max out at six years apart. The REAL kicker is I LOOK NOTHING LIKE our father but my siblings??? ...nearly spitting images of him. See, you're already thinking, well? Are you?! (LOL) I know, it's human nature, really. Truth is, I was told our dad was a writing, poetic machine. How cool is it that I am a writer?! The day came, and I didn't care anymore that people had an opinion. I decided to be at peace with ME. I'm here now, right? YOUR GIRL IS ON THE SCENE, kickin' tail and takin' names! I decided since I was already on my way somewhere, it might as well be on to GREATNESS! ...to be cont'd.

~

May 14, 2013

Friends don't let friends go through life WITHOUT encouragement and inspiration! Help me live my dream by sharing my <3 in hopes of helping others overcome their fears, their painful pasts, and their own self-sabotage!

...."if I can see it, than I can do it, IF I just believe it, there's nothing to it, I BELIEVE I CAN FLY, I believe I can touch the sky, I think about it every night and day....(you take it from here and wave your hands in the air while you sing it!!!!!) AND

BELIEVE IN YOURSELF!!!!! You can do it, you can MAKE IT!!!! Hold on. *Don't you dare give up!!!* I'm routing for you!!

~

MAY 16, 2013

Daily dying to self is such a great gift. I used to believe that doing what I DIDN'T want to do was punishment. Then I realized it was such an immature response - like a two-year old screaming in a temper tantrum! We have all heard someone say, "I don't FEEL like it, or I don't FEEL like doing that!!" When you realize that your feelings can go from one level to the exact opposite in a split second (depending on the circumstance), you will see that you LACK maturity when you have a TEMPER TANTRUM and you don't get your way! Wisdom and self-control speak volumes when you and others see YOU GET WORK DONE!!! When the work of your hands PRODUCES RESULTS time and time again, maturity is added to your character.

Do the hard part - PRESS THROUGH, live OUTSIDE of your feelings and inside a DO-RIGHT MINDSET! #GROWup #GetRESULTS #beMATURE

~

MAY 21, 2013

I remember when life was so cruel!!! One time in particular, I, with my two beautiful babies, had to move to a homeless shelter and bathe with reclaimed water for nearly SIX weeks (and boy does it STINK). I was at the lowest of lows - financially, spiritually and physically. I really didn't know how I would rebuild my life and the lives of these two precious and innocent little girls......BUT GOD KNEW!

I resolved to NEVER accept domestic violence again in my

life and never to be used and abused by another soul, EVER, in life. Though I was at my lowest in so many ways, I STOOD TALLER and prouder than I ever had in my 25 years of life! I felt like a GIANT!

Have you ever been so down that you couldn't even recognize yourself? I cried and cried night after night once I put my babies to sleep. I couldn't believe what I had done to my life!!!! Low self-esteem, childhood abuse, and not knowing "my place" is how I got there - but then there's the RESTART button. What a FABU-LOUS time to leave your past right where it is and begin again! I absolutely HATED myself for making such asinine decisions that landed me and my babies in such a poor place in life. Not only was I affected, but two innocent little people were in tow. YET, I started over. REFRESHED. RENEWED. DETERMINED with a mind to NOT EVER GO BACK TO THAT PLACE. One day at a time. One decision at a time - not perfect but determined. And since that time, I haven't made dumb decisions like those that landed me where I was. It's an awesome thing to look back and NOT wonder how I got over. I know FULL WELL HOW and WHO GOT ME OVER: God, me, and faith - the three amigos (lol). GET THIS: God is truly good, but sometimes God cannot do a thing UNLESS we move our hands, feet and heart, by faith. A LOT. EVERYDAY. If you agree, hit the LIKE button and share my story to encourage somebody today! He's done so much for me, I cannot tell it all!!!!

～

MAY 21, 2013

On my business cards I have the acronym, HLIC: meaning HEAD LADY in CHARGE. When I got the gist of what that meant, EVERYTHING changed. I had to realize that many of the trials I was facing was because of my LACK of understanding that I was the one in charge of my destiny!!!! Speak a word of encouragement to YOURSELF. Pop ya collar and walk with a pep in your step!!!! You deserve to be celebrated! If you survived another day without going back to where you started, that is a great reason to celebrate. CELEBRATE your growth and accomplishments. Enjoy your newfound maturity and peace. It was you who did the work, the studying, and the crazy schedules. YOU endured the hardships and lack. Are you better than you were six months ago, a year ago, even a month ago??? Lead the way! Celebrate the "God in you"!

~

MAY 21, 2013

In the midnight hour of life, if you don't have the hope that morning is on the way, you start believing the wrong hype. You start believing the negative in your head: Things like, "my life will never change, I'll never get out of this rut, no one loves me, I cannot do anything but what I'm doing now".......WHAT A LIE! Don't believe what the denouncer says. You know he comes to steal, kill and destroy your very soul!!!!!

Change your mind, it is yours for God's sake! Life and an ABUNDANT one is yours for the asking, working and living. Do not purposely live BENEATH your privilege. Don't be wasteful. Turn on the light of HOPE! It's in you. USE IT, fully and completely! FILL YOUR CUP TO OVERFLOWING. *So many* need your EXTRA!

~

MAY 21, 2013

Odd Ball In: Part 2

Married, with my baby girl, we left Eglin AFB, Goodfellow AFB in San Angelo, TX, and traveled up the east coast to say good bye to family as we headed for our new life together - not in another state, but in another country, for crying out loud. We were headed for the beautiful city of Bedfordshire, England, just about 50 minutes from London, England to Royal Air Force Chicksands. The eight-hour flight was surreal. I cried with excitement while we watched movies and our baby girl, Lexy, colored in coloring book after coloring book.

I could hardly believe the beautiful life we were experiencing: Driving on the left side of the road, riding the TUBE from city to city, eating the REAL fish & chips, riding up top on the double decker bus while touring Buckingham Palace, Trafalgar Square, Robinhood's World (VERY beautiful, by the way), and so many other incredibly stunning castles. The only thing I HATED was the numerous trips to the E.R.: Face bruises, kicked in my ribs so hard that I just knew they were broken, a dislocated shoulder that I PROMISED the doctors came from me falling down the stairs, for the second time. THREE TIMES in 18 months I made these trips to the hospital. ODDly enough, I thought it was best to "love my location" rather than love my life. Fair enough trade, right? I refused to go back to the life I had already lived through: Horrific childhood abuse, constant rejection, lack on so many levels...I somehow thought that what I'd been through as a child and where I was as an adult were FAR different from each other. Then, I got a revelation - I COULD FIGHT BACK! I COULD STAND UP FOR MYSELF! As a child, I wasn't covered. Abuse was rampant. ODDly enough, I didn't know that I, me, little bitty ole me, could TAKE A STAND and demand respect for myself. Things changed when I learned the LIFE breathing truth of SPEAKING UP. I was beginning to be OKAY with being the TINY but MIGHTY one. What a day of rejoicing it was when I heard the reverberation of my own voice taking a stand against any more pain!

"Still that hope that lies within is reassured as I keep my eyes upon the distant shore. I know He'll lead me safely to that blessed place He has prepared, but if the storms don't cease and the winds keep on blowing in my life, my soul has been anchored in the Lord."

To be cont'd...

~

MAY 21, 2013

I'm not ashamed anymore. The longer I kept it all in my heart and soul, the more this ENORMOUS cloud of shame and disgrace stayed within me. I became sick and tired of being out of balance. I looked good on the exterior, but I was wounded and broken on the inside. That was then. And the half has NOT even been told. So much more coming soon!

~

MAY 22, 2013

GET UP and move somethin'! How will your circumstance change if all you do is "watch and pray?" My grandmother used to say, "Weight broke down the bridge!"(lol) How heavy will your situation have to get before YOU take the first step into your destiny? How many more people can you complain to? How many more hours of doing nothing will you waste? Who else can you blame for what happened back then? The road TO the blessed place is just as beautiful and important as the "LIFE CHANGING" moment. DECIDE. TODAY. UP and at 'em, baby cakes! Your beautiful life is waiting!

~

MAY 23, 2013

Keep your eyes on the prize!!!

LET no thing.......childhood trauma, poverty, pain, debt, divorce, unforgiveness, domestic violence, unemployment, death, betrayal, depression, OPPRESSION, NOT ONE THING, separate you from meeting your goals.

Just know that distractions are a part of the journey! Realize what distractions are WORTH putting your dreams on hold. Some of the irritants come to KEEP you off course permanently. Those irritants could be clothed in the everyday, mundane, comfortable place of home and work. Challenge yourself to deal with the distractions then GET BACK AT IT!

~

May 25, 2013

I will always hope, always believe things will get better, and always have faith that God has something in store for me that is ABSOLUTELY phenomenal! Having your own priorities in the right order allows you to say yes or no when your support is needed by others. Share your time and space but make sure you share it for the things that make your life richer and fuller.

Don't say yes just because you were asked. Say yes because you have something great to give!

~

May 30, 2013

Looking inward means dealing with the hard parts of our own lives. So many times, it is us - we are our own worst enemy. We doubt ourselves, so we doubt others. We don't trust ourselves, so we surely cannot trust another.

Look inward and purge.......purge all the crud that's held you back for decades. FREE YOURSELF to <3 and LIVE LARGE!

Everyday should be SWEETER than the day before.

Let's get to the lovely part of life that was created for us! Don't let your living be in vain. Uplift, encourage, SET THE STANDARD, smile, forgive, BE AT PEACE.

Start the journey from within...get to the GOOD PART!!!!

~

MAY 30, 2013

Starting is so UNDER-rated. Go ahead and give yourself some props for making the biggest STEP to your blessed place! Pat your own self on the back for moving on IN SPITE of your fears, feelings of insecurity and the negativity going on in your head!!!! YOU DID IT!

You have strength inside you that YOU aren't even aware of. You will find this beautiful strength when you DO what scares the hell out of you! Your heart will feel like it's jumping out of your chest, but.....YOU GOT THE HARDEST PART DONE. Now keep going - don't you dare stop there. When you keep moving forward IN SPITE OF the crud, perseverance and peace meet up with faith and fulfillment! You will look back and SEE yourself in a whole new light – confidence shows UP! This life-style is CONTAGIOUS and very good for the soul!

~

MAY 30, 2013

When I believe I can, I do. When I believe I can't, I don't. Your life accepts what your mind believes. Winners do what every quitter refuses to!

~

JUNE 2, 2013

You ever hear God saying, "Not this time, go this way", and your flesh is so used to going another? Yet, the still, small voice of his presence gives you a peace that cannot be explained, and you do the new thing. That happened to me today, and all I can say is

THANK YOU, LORD for being concerned about every little, tiny thing that concerns me. People, we must live the life we sing, talk and write about. Many times, it's not the loud, IN YOUR FACE "sign" that gives us direction. Often, we need to take a deep breath, refuse to react immediately, and DO ABSOLUTELY NOTHING....no-thing. Write the vision, research the concept, ignite our faith and BE FOUND WAITING when the answer manifests. We have to be still and know that God is who he says He is. Being still and waiting is so absolutely difficult at times. Waiting is a part of the process of growing and maturing our souls to do nothing when we are ready (or so we think), to take off and GO. Doing nothing, my friends, takes IMMEASURABLE FAITH.

~

JUNE 10, 2013

The greatest you the world has ever seen is WAITING ON YOU to make a move! Get in the game, lovely people!!!! How long will you stand on the sidelines and TALK about what you WILL do to accomplish your dream?

Goals and strategies are the TOOLS you will use, yet strength, courage and wisdom are the CHARACTERISTICS you MUST HAVE!

"You cannot see the picture if you're inside the frame!" ~Les Brown

~

JUNE 10, 2013

I remember being a kid and ABSOLUTELY hated my life! Days turned into weeks, weeks turned into months and months turned into years of HATING MY LIFE! No matter what I was doing, it never failed, there was a huge void in my life - so many nearly debilitating broken pieces in every area of my life, from childhood into young adulthood. As soon as "I got the memo" that I had a POWERFUL VOICE within me, I changed so many things about my life. I realized that everything I needed to be an incredibly beautiful force in the earth realm WAS ALREADY INSIDE OF ME. I believed what I read and heard about my purpose! I made it personal. I finally took OWNERSHIP of my role and responsibilities for my life! Celebrate good times, come on!

~

June 10, 2013

Poverty, rape, a history of family drug abuse, and the child abuse I endured were all tools to help me pray for DEATH. I died weekly, sometimes daily during my formative years. I would lie down at night and PRAY to God, "Please God, please don't wake me up in the morning!" When you see me now, LIVING FREE and filled with JOY, it is because I decided to LIVE apart from what was placed upon me as a child. I replaced all that abuse, depression and anger with peace, joy and dreams fulfilled! I am a VICTORIOUS WOMAN because I made a decision that I would be in charge!!! I choose this life every day, MAKING SURE my future is a testimony, in spite of my past!

Believing in yourself is the best GIFT you can receive. Why do I say that? People can speak life to you until you are blue in the face, but get this, UNTIL YOU, yourself, BELIEVE those inspiring words and OWN them, it does not matter what great words you hear or what wonderful books you read. If you cannot receive inspiration as your own, it does not matter what the greatest motivator on earth can say to you.

Believe you are PHENOMENAL and life will bring you opportunities to give back in a phenomenal way.

OUT with the negative self-talk, IN with "I WAS BORN TO

CREATE WEALTH": A wealth of love, peace, laughter, forgiveness, grace, joy and so much more. I've also found that you REAP what you SOW! ;-) Reaping all of the above is truly a blessing but giving the same....now that is PRICELESS.

I believe in the power of prayer drenched in faith! I believe there is more good in the world than evil. I believe I was created to be a LIGHT in dark places. I believe that hard work and starting over after things don't go as planned, bring you to a point in life where you have to decide to learn from your experiences or decide to quit. I've come to this place countless times in my 41 years. Each time, I decided to move forward.

Failure isn't in my vocabulary, for even when the plans DIDN'T work out, what I chose to bring WITH ME is MORE than what I knew before! MORE wisdom, knowledge and understanding than any person could have told me, and more than what I could have learned in a classroom.

So please, don't quit on people or yourself. Learn from the hard, hurtful places and decide that you're a winner because your <3 determines your MARK! Take the blessings of learning and leave the bitterness of resentment.

∼

June 11, 2013

Make the effort, put in the work. Your life is worth every second of getting to the other side of pain! How many of you know that FREEdom ain't free, it costs us something!!! Happy Tuesday, beautiful people!

My oldest sister was diagnosed with epilepsy this morning. She will have a long recovery because she fell on her shoulder and legs pretty hard and bit her tongue all the way through. I'm sad, but I have more hope and faith than sadness. It's tough being so far away from home right now.

When stuff gets crazy like this, I get to praying!!! I believe in the One who delivered me from some of the most heinous abuse! On top of that, He delivered me from a heart filled with hate in the worst way. It's this same Lord that I believe in who will restore my sister: Spirit, soul and body!!!

❧

June 12, 2013

I cannot even begin to tell you how awesome it is to live and breathe with a heart of hope! I flipped the script on hopelessness and depression and began creating pleasant and joy-filled memories! I had to create enough beautiful ones to overshadow all the crud-filled ones.

I am pleased to announce He gives beauty for ashes, strength for fear, gladness for mourning and peace for despair. Don't be afraid to begin again. I did, and I haven't looked back since!

Happy Wednesday, beautiful people!

❧

June 13, 2013

Take the beautiful thing that you know about yourself and use that to help somebody. Whatever it is - charity, sincerity, a hug, ears that will KEEP a secret, even wisdom. When asked, give it. JUST move forward with what is already beautiful instead of complaining about what is NOT right with who you are. If you share what is already good with you, what you think is not so good will be worked out! Why? Helping others is a down payment for your own life's rewards.

❧

June 14, 2013

What you feel and what you believe are VERY, VERY different. Some would say, "I feel like I'm supposed to say this or do that." Others say, "I believe with everything in my being that I am supposed to do this!" The difference is what we "feel" can and does change by the moment. Sometimes, what we BELIEVE is something deeper down in our souls. It is consistent. What we BELIEVE has the STAYING POWER to bring about consistent work. Consistent work brings about manifestation because it is not dependent upon emotions. It is dependent upon the goal!!! TRUTH+CONSISTENCY=MANIFESTATION

~

June 14, 2013

Overwhelmed with joy right now. It took 30 years, but I did it! I pushed beyond my fears and what I thought may happen, and I DID IT!

I called my Dad's brother whom I have never seen or spoken to. I was the "white" sheep of my dad's side of the family and wasn't well accepted at all. It hurt deeply for all these years. I looked at the phone number in my phone for what seemed like an hour, but it was just seconds. Before I knew it, I hit the CALL button!!!!!!!! I asked to speak with Antonio, aka Tony. He obviously looked at his caller ID and saw the city/state because he said, "Oh my Lord, THIS IS MY NIECE, Lisa, isn't it?" His excitement took me by surprise. All I could do was cry.

~

June 15, 2013

If you want to make it to the top, you MUST PUT IN THE WORK and keep doing that! Even if others GET you to the top, in order to stay there, YOU MUST PUT YOUR HANDS TO THE PLOW! What in the FREE WORLD are you waiting on beautiful people? Get up and invest in your future! The hard work you put in **today** will be your incredible blessing **tomorrow**!

~

JUNE 18, 2013

The best thing to do when you are overwhelmed and frustrated is eat ice cream (LOL). Then, watch a funny movie like "What About Bob".

I promise you, this has been one of my top remedies for almost 10 years! Laughter is good like medicine! It will change your whole outlook on life and your particular situation. In other words, don't take yourself so seriously, you probably need to lighten up anyway. Life is short, then you die. Don't die sad, frustrated and disgusted.

Die happy and peacefully.

So, go ahead, yes, right now, go to the freezer and have ice cream for breakfast, then go to YouTube and watch What About Bob!

:-) You will thank me later. Happy Tuesday, beautiful people!

~

JUNE 23, 2013

Here today, gone today. Life and death can happen in an instant! Don't live with heart wrenching guilt and unforgiveness. If you FULLY realize that at ANY GIVEN MOMENT you could take your last breath, you may be inspired enough to change a few things. Be the first to free yourself and apologize, more for the sake of peace than anything else. YOUR peace is something you should protect. Kill your pride and allow the freedom of joy and peace to replace it. It's worth it, I promise.

~

June 24, 2013

Be the mature one and allow your child(ren) their right to spend quality time with your ex. Don't pawn your children because your ex moved on with someone else. Our babies deserve better. Maturity shows itself best in the face of opposition and tough times. If you're hurt, deal with that and don't mix YOUR emotions with the fact that your ex is a good parent. They need the non-custodial parent just as much as they need you. Your children will rise up and call you blessed because you were wise and mature enough to NOT confuse the two. Children need both parents. If the absent parent makes the effort to co-parent, do what is right, and allow it to happen. Our children need ALL THE LOVE they can get from their parents.

It's a mean, mean world out there. Our babies need to know they are WELL-LOVED by both Mom and Dad and any BONUS parent who may enter the picture. When your child(ren) get older and look back on it all, may they remember you as the blessing, not the curse.

~

July 3, 2013

Perspective ALERT!!!!

- 15-year-old beautiful young lady at my daughter's high school - just buried a week ago.
- 39-year-old director of nursing, single mother of one son - buried a week ago.
- 1-year-old baby boy - services this week.

... and people live with bitterness, hearts filled with resentment and jealousy, no thankfulness in their hearts, nothing checked off their "bucket list". As a matter of fact, you don't even have a BUCKET LIST! YOU, YES YOU, can be here today and

GONE today! Don't think any of us are the exception to the rule. Come on people, life is beautiful WHEN YOU REALIZE IT! Let's make your life lovely and peaceful in the midst of all the pain and struggle. If you need help, be excited enough to ask for it! If you only knew what is waiting on your stinkin' thinking.

~

July 3, 2013

Some folks are just ABUNDANTLY blessed with gifts - so many that they don't even use them all in one year! How about this: The gifts you're sitting on, or are going unused, share with someone else. Sing at a nursing home, give free child care to a single mom one night a week, create a bouquet for a sick neighbor, create a painting for someone you know who is need of encouragement, or pen a rhyme and make it an art piece. The list could go on and on! Your gift should be poured out, not hidden or kept under lock and key. Our lives are richer and fuller and more ALIVE when we SHARE OUR GIFTS and TALENTS.

~

July 10, 2013

Migraines are truly from the very pit of hell! After battling since Saturday night, I got my life back today - and I am so very grateful! Grateful to be able to hold up my head, clean my house, and listen to music. When we casually live day after day, the things I just mentioned become common place to us. We take life for granted.

We have to be careful. Good health and a sound mind are TRUE blessings.

~

JULY 29, 2013

Take the pressure off from yourself. When you don't know how to solve the problem, just be OKAY with it and say, "I DON'T KNOW." Then pray about it, seek wisdom for your answer and/or ASK FOR HELP. Be alright with NOT having all the answers. We're human. We don't know all the answers. Sometimes, we need to just say, "Peace, be still" and let that do it.

~

AUGUST 8, 2013

I had a TRUE "I'm thankful for the simple things" moment last night. My days and nights run right into each other, but lately I've been intentional about being PRESENT, especially with my two youngest daughters being back home from summer vacation. Running water, electricity, food other than mayo and mustard sandwiches, a washer and dryer instead of washing loads of clothes in the bathtub with Dial soap - let me tell you how thankful I am today. I am so grateful that...

I PREACH TO MY KIDS to let them know how truly blessed they are. Many of our kids are CLUELESS to the struggles that their peers have to endure.

TEACH THEM WELL. SHARE with them how far you've come. Get them to understand that WE WORK HARD, so they can do the very same thing and reap the benefits. TESTIFY about the goodness of the Lord because faith AND works are how it is done. If you, too, are an overcomer, let your babies know the truth of what you have overcome. Your pride may instill in them a false sense of security. Let your children know how strong in faith you are. Let them know they come from good stock, from a family of hard working, faith-walking overcomers! Allow the truth to bless them.

~

AUGUST 12, 2013

There are SEVEN days in a week and SOMEDAY is not one of them. Fail to plan and plan to fail. Write the vision and MOVE FORWARD toward your destiny.

~

AUGUST 21, 2013

You ever feel down and out? Sometimes lonely and overwhelmed, then a friend or co-worker calls with a situation TEN TIMES WORSE than yours???? You end up talking them through their situation and FEEL BETTER YOURSELF!

Helping others helps us!

~

AUGUST 22, 2013

Live your life so well that when you die, all people will be able to say is SHE/HE didn't have an ounce left to give!!!! So, GIVE IT YOUR ALL. EVERYDAY. LEAVE NOTHING ON THE TABLE. Be grateful for the time you are given. Do something wonderful with your life!

~

AUGUST 29, 2013

Some people are so rich all they have is M O N E Y!!! Be rich in wisdom, love, peace, forgiveness and kindness. You will go a MILLION times further than any amount of money ever will.

Don't believe me? Ask the thousands of FORMER millionaires who won the lottery five years ago but are now DIRT POOR. If you don't already own it in your soul, no amount of money will ever get you there. Financial abundance is the bonus to a heart filled with goodness!

~

SEPTEMBER 12, 2013

Know your child(ren) so well that even if they don't say a word, YOU KNOW when something is wrong!!!! Don't allow the world and all the infiltrations to take you away from ONE of your most important roles – a parent. No job, no person, place or thing is EVER as important as KNOWING FULL WELL when your child is hurting. You may not be able to FIX every situation but KNOW who will. Their lives depend on us!

~

SEPTEMBER 12, 2013

When giving is your very nature, make sure your giving is wrapped in WISDOM! Be careful and make sure you're surrounded by people who will help you keep HEALTHY boundaries. You can be yourself and give, just be aware of the TAKERS. God gave you POWER, LOVE and a SOUND MIND as well - so, yes, utilize ALL the gifts! ;-) Happy COOL Thursday, beautiful people!

~

SEPTEMBER 20, 2013

Things, people and even the air we breathe change. Be okay with that. But, never, ever be OKAY with being stagnate. That is the place where life can become funky. A stench begins when stillness happens, just like the lack of oxygen creates a very bad odor when water stops flowing. Mentally and spiritually we begin to HATE on folks who are working their own lane and living their dreams while you sit back and look confused. Movement, wise methodical movement, prevents stagnation. Clarity and a well-laid-out plan will help you get moving in the right direction. Remember, a pause is VERY, VERY different than a lifetime of being STUCK!

～

September 20, 2013

Enter in and stay in the race. We all get tired, discouraged and down-right irritable. Rest can help us get back in the right mood and frame of mind. Rest helps us get our mind in good working order. BE okay with that time of rest that you need, then GET BACK IN THERE! Your destination is just up the road a bit so, keep making progress. Even if it's a tiny bit of progress, remember, you are not STUCK. A win is a win, whether by one point or by 50 - it all goes down the same. Call forth victory and do it consistently. Happy Friday, VICTORIOUS people!

～

December 10, 2013

I heard a story of a man who was abandoned by his mother on the corner of a street when he was 3 years old! He STAYED there for THREE DAYS before anyone helped him. Today, that man is nearly 65 years old, and a COMMITTED advocate and VOICE for abandoned and impoverished children all over the world. I wonder when he was growing up as a young child, if he ever dreamed or imagined he would be WHERE HE IS and doing such a life-changing work for "the least of those".

His setback was a setup for a COME-BACK! At some point, he took ownership of his life and set goals for his future! He decided to create what he wanted AND to bring many, many, many babies with him! He decided to embrace the very things that could have destroyed his life. He somehow found that in the midst of his pain, feelings of abandonment and rejection, that there was STILL a DIVINE purpose for his life!

37

What a teachable moment! Question: How much more can you blame "them" or continue to live in the past as painful as it was? Time is moving right along while the present time is continually waiting patiently for you to get over it! Heal and make your life count for something beautiful! Resentment binds you even more than what happened to you! FREEDOM, forgiveness and walking in your PURPOSE is your PAYBACK on your past!

"Where you came from may be someone else's doing - where you go from here is TOTALLY UP TO YOU!"

-Lisa Sunshine

~

December 11, 2013

I tell you what, if it ain't one thing it's two, and guess what? LIFE KEEPS MOVING! While you're wallowing, whining and blaming, life is still moving. Goals still need to be accomplish-ed, and you have a choice - to be defeated or defeat the issue. Rise up and live, regardless of what bad news you receive! Every day won't be easy, and it isn't supposed to be. Choose to know and believe that no one has a perfect life. Be alright with that and know that TROUBLE DON'T LAST ALWAYS! Get you some peace and prayer time, some great inspirational music and choose peace vs turmoil in your heart. Your turmoil, your "night season" COULD be a future blessing if you choose to learn while going through it. How you move through the chaos is surely UP TO YOU. What a tremendous gift, the gift of choice!

~

December 12, 2013

Happy Thursday, lovely people!

The spirit of giving must be captured at a very early age.

Giving of your time, your space, your listening ear or sometimes a few dollars here and there are great ways to change your funky mood!

Give to a loved one or many times, a total stranger. It will change your whole outlook on situations - not for you to brag about it, but to live knowing you gave to someone who will probably never, EVER pay you back! Grab an angel from the Angel Tree in the mall. As a family or group of co-workers, adopt a family for Christmas.

Parents: Be the example that your children need to see. Yes, there are children who grow up and do JUST THE OPPOSITE of what you taught them, but the majority WATCH us more than they listen. Take heed - THEY ARE WATCH-ING, even when you think they aren't. What I'm merely saying is charity begins at home. Share it and live it.

My prayer is that you will give of yourself in some way during this Christmas season and receive the blessings of sharing that opportunity with the young people in your life. Start a GIVING legacy with your family. There's no time like the present. (pun intended) ;-)

The End.

AFTERWORD

P.S. - Thank you for taking the time to learn a little more about me. It took me several years to heal and get to the core of WHY God created me. There were so many days when I asked God why I was created, but I didn't get the response I wanted. I wanted God to kill everyone who had ever hurt me. That is how deep the pain was that I couldn't shake. Coping mechanisms became the vices that held me together when I wanted to just give up on life. I wanted to heal quickly and forget about all that happened to me. I wanted all my bad decisions to go away. Of course, you know God wouldn't have cheated me out of a very powerful recovery process.

What about you? How powerful is your story? How many people need to hear your voice and how you overcame the shame, guilt and pain of your past?

www.ingramcontent.com/pod-product-compliance
Lightning Source LLC
Chambersburg PA
CBHW031935080426
42734CB00007B/701